TO BECOMING
MY OWN CAPTAIN

To Becoming; My Own Captain

Irene Mugure Nderitu

Published by Irene Mugure Nderitu, 2023.

TO BECOMING; MY OWN CAPTAIN

First edition. April 18, 2023.

Copyright © 2023 Irene Mugure Nderitu.

ISBN: 979-8223683643

Written by Irene Mugure Nderitu.

To God, for the gift of life, for His mercy, for His compassion and for His unconditional love.

To my dad, the Late Paul Mwangi Nderitu, for being a loving role model, mentor and friend.

To my beautiful daughter, Lisa Wabai Nderitu, for being a wonderful gift, an inspiration and for helping me relearn what life is all about.

Introduction

A m seated at what should be my furnished living room area but with nothing that resembles a furnished living room. Again and again pondering over "who am I, why am I here, how did I get here, what happened, where it all happened and when the rain started beating". Am shipwrecked. For a lack of a better word.

To say am overwhelmed would be an understatement. A series of events in the past few years have left me knocked down and now on survival mode. A common joke would suffice, that it was all part of life's character development. Life happens and you are left reeling from the aftershocks. When you have to readjust the sails. When the storm hits and before you can gather your wits, are hard on the floor. What is left of you is a product of life. Initially, in unbelief, denial, shock and sickly. Only not in hospital.

Maybe you have been there. You then try to pick yourself up, and if lucky, still have some fiber of strength to trudge on the dusty road of life. Not in a cast but wearing a mask, wondering what next.

Life happens they say. And when life hands you lemons, make lemonade. Question is, should life just happen? Do we allow life to happen? Is there no way we can be intentional and deliberate from the get go to avoid some of the pitfalls we encounter? Shouldn't there be a manual. A book of wisdom. A curriculum to prep and guide on how to maneuver through life.

Take for instance a business, which ideally should have a life of its own, we are deliberate and intentional over the undertaking. Often having taken a basic business course on how to run a business.

We learn that there needs to be a purpose to the business. A vision. A mission. Values attached to the business. A brand. A positioning statement. A value statement and a road map to achieve its key objectives. A qualified team to oversee its successful execution.

Question begs, shouldn't one on the same merit be purposeful, intentional and deliberate in their personal life? I then begin to interrogate. What course should I have taken on life? What is my purpose? What is my vision, my mission, my value system, my personal brand, my road map to success and qualified team to ensure success?

A lot has been said on purpose, vision, mission, values and personal success. Ultimately, how do we measure success? And just like the business, I continue to interrogate, who am I? Why am I here? What do I do? Who do I serve, how do I serve, where and when.

Who am I

Who am I without the titles, roles and or hats that I wear. Who am I without the earthly possessions?

Jesus asked a similar question. In Mathew 16:13-17, "Who do people say the Son of Man is?" They replied, "Some say John the Baptist, others say Elijah, Jeremiah or one of the prophets." "But what about you?" he asked. "Who do you say I am?" Simon Peter answered, "You are the Messiah, the son of the living God."

Jesus replied, "Blessed are you, Simon son of Jonah, for this was not revealed to you by flesh and blood, but my Father in heaven."

The people had different opinions of who Jesus was but it was not the truth. Likewise, someone's opinion of me does not have to be my reality. I am different, unique and have my own, one of a kind thumbprint. Am an original and not a perfect copy of someone else. A product of God's workmanship. A masterpiece. I am wonderfully and fearfully made. I am made in God's image. A child of the highest God.

My identity should not be pegged on the world's opinion, titles, possessions, race, tribe, cultural beliefs, socialization, social expectations, family background, educational background, professional qualifications, marital status, roles, my past, relationships and or social media standing. However, we always find ourselves trying to get validation and affirmation from others. Thus acting out the social expectations to appease everyone but our intrinsic selves.

Ideally, when I know who I am, I should not have to remind people who I am based on the external. I should be clothed in self-worth and humility just like Jesus. Clothed in self-value, self-respect and love.

Evidently Jesus knew His identity as the son of the living God. In John 13:3, we witness Jesus who identifies Himself as a servant leader and Messiah. Hence, He did not hesitate to wash the disciples' feet and take the form of a servant leader. Peter simply could not comprehend it, as he found it such a lowly thing to have Jesus, the perceived master and leader wash the disciples' feet. Jesus however went ahead to wash the disciples' feet because He knew who He was. He was secure in His identity.

Further, Jesus went ahead to offer Himself as the living sacrifice to fulfill the will of God. Similarly, if one is secure in their own identity, they will partake in whatever they purpose to do without hesitation and without seeking external validation.

However, a lot of us are lost and misguided because we subscribe to what people have to say about us, the expectations, the labels put on us by the society, the opinions of others instead of what God has to say about us. Thus allowing the opinions of others to rob us of our authentic self-identity and purpose.

Thus ignoring, knowingly or unknowingly the fact that an individual's true identity is who they are at the core and not what is perceived by others. The good book warns us not to conform to the ways of the world, as well inscribed in Romans 12, "Do not conform any longer to the pattern of this world, but be transformed by the renewing of your mind. Then you will be able to test and approve what God's will is, His good, pleasing and perfect will".

Most, if not all of us, unfortunately struggle with self-identity and self-expression. May explain the self-doubt and lack of confidence to undertake our dreams, desires and or will of God as evidenced by Moses. For when Moses was called on to deliver the Israelites, he asked God whom he should say had sent him as he regarded himself lowly in relation to the Pharaoh whom he was required to address.

In Exodus 3:14, God said to Moses, "I AM WHO I AM". This is what you are to say to the Israelites: I AM has sent me to you".

Granted, seeing that we are said to be made in God's image, shouldn't we on the same merit be "I am who I am" regardless of my status and or circumstances?

That said, what was my understanding of who I am? On the other hand, how has world opinion and social expectation shaped my self-identity?

In retrospect, I may have allowed my wounded self and or concern over public opinion, lead me astray and or distract me from my authentic self, identity and purpose. Fear of not matching up to the societal expectations and being labelled a failure.

Evidently our inner conversations, battle in the mind, conflicted beliefs, manifest in our own story and reflect in our self-value. Hence the need to interrogate our inner conversations and beliefs that we have of ourselves. The plan being to make our desired story be conformed to God's will, plan and purpose for our lives. Arguably, our authentic self. Our intended purpose, place and plan.

To make our story happen and not to let life happen to us, taking into account that it is often said that there are those that make things happen, others watch as things happen and others who simply don't know what happened.

My Story

The common understanding is that you don't ask a lady how old she is. Personally, I like to think of myself as sixteen years old plus years of life experience, sold out to Jesus Christ, a single mother of one beautiful daughter and bearing an entrepreneurial spirit.

However, am conflicted and at crossroads. Some may want to call it a midlife crisis. And maybe it is. A time to reflect. A time of introspection. My current situation starkly reminding me that all is not well.

How did I get here? My childhood days were not perfect but bearable. Sailed through primary school and went on to a nationally ranked high school. So far had it all pretty much figured out. So I thought. So where did I get it wrong? In hindsight, a series of bad choices, lack of guidance, lack of purpose, ignorance and or naivety. Thus my firm belief that life skills and guidance on purpose should be incorporated into the educational system to prep one for the life ahead. A honing of self-identity and skillset should also be emphasized.

Previously, in the African culture, it was the mandate of the tribe to prep youngsters for the life ahead. Over time, the culture has been abandoned, leaving youngsters to practically adult themselves, with sometimes catastrophic results.

In contrast to my childhood days, my adult life has been full of drama to say the least. Well, according to the public script. Amazing how many scripts and narratives can be written about an individual. Depending on whom you ask, their opinion and or perspective will be different. Again depending on whom you ask, the story will largely depend on the information they may have and or from whom they got their information. Was it direct or an indirect source? Whether the information was from one side of the coin or both sides of the coin. Whether objective or biased. Whether it was an ill coined narrative or well-intended narrative. Whether the information was validated or was is it a story of the broken telephone.

That said, knowing that I could not trust the people around me to be a reliable source of information nor myself to honestly answer who I am and what is my story, I turn to God, "Who do you say I am?

It is a time such as this that am grateful that I got to learn the word of God at an opportune time. Prior to the desert experience. The Word has helped me in my life's journey and has guided me through the different seasons of life.

Nonetheless, my heart is screaming. Fighting for dear life to say the least. While barely holding onto the shreds of faith and hope still left in me.

So begins a journey of exploration while struggling to keep afloat. Again, where did the rain start beating? If I could turn back the clock, what should my younger self have known? Should I have sat through a class that could have helped me unpack what life was truly about?

All I remember, was the all too familiar narrative and or socialization that one should go through school, get good grades, get a good job and everything else would fall into place. A good house, a flashy car and a beautiful family to boot.

Therefore, like all else, I went through school with that single mind set and expectation of what would follow past my school life. However, a number of gaps were left out from the said common narrative. That some issues in life are not text book material per se. Mainly, I was lacking in wisdom. Wisdom that should have been shared and passed on through generations.

Hence, for the most part, life played out against a backdrop of ignorance while trying my best to match up to societal expectation albeit with a few hits and misses along the way. Arguably, I was lucky to have had it all seemingly figured it out, until lady luck ran out and the enemy came knocking.

A casual phrase often thrown around is that, if one does not meet up with the enemy along life's journey, chances are, you are walking in the same direction with the enemy. Hence, with daggers drawn and fingers pointing at me, the battle arena is set. With many of the spectators unfamiliar with the nitty gritty details and events leading up to my current situation, save only for the all-knowing powerful God.

A storm brews up. The persons around gladly partaking in the fray, confusion and condemnation. The arrows come, fast and furious. Where is my companion? Where is my prince? Where is my shield? Where is my rock? I cry out. The Alpha and Omega. I sigh. Is this my battle or God's battle?

Battling against myself, society and or God. Battling against expectations of myself, society and God. Daring to go against the tide and stereotypes. For in essence, from the get go, my story is already scripted and rated against a given societal yardstick. Wherever I go, the story is already transcribed and rated against my family background, family expectations, religion, tribe, country, gender, educational background, professional qualification, possessions, marital status, relationships, associations, social standing and or business.

Anything short of the societal expectation and standards set is thus scorned at, considered a failure and a misfit by society. The consensus being, that one should follow the cultural norms of society.

A general template of what your story should churn out to be having been crafted early on and expected to be played along. I am therefore expected to conduct myself in a certain manner, limited to the societal belief system, culture, norms and confined to life's chromos.

My inner voice and or critic constantly reminding me of the script. My inner conversation bellowing when I excelled and booing when I failed to follow through the said script. The society was not kind either, only too happy to magnify the scorecard. The pressure is on.

It is no wonder, that our stories are more or less a manifestation of the societal expectations and inner conversations. Fortunately, and or unfortunately, in conformity with a character laid out by society. The princess or the slave girl.

Question begs, if you are a societal character, what have you resigned yourself to? Given the chance, what script would you write for yourself and most importantly what script has God written for you? Would your story be shaped by societal norms and expectations? Is there a mismatch between what the society expects of you and your inner desire? Is there a mismatch between what God's script is of you and your story? Whose agenda am I fulfilling? Am I fulfilling God's agenda, societal agenda and or own agenda?

Should I conform to a certain narrative, expectation or can I rewrite my own script? Can I drop the stories, narratives and labels placed upon me? Can I be the leading lady in my own story? The star of the show. In sync with God's purpose and will for my life.

Shipwrecked

If I had known better, my story would probably have been different. Leading a more organized, disciplined and purposeful life. Ideally, an independent, confident, healthy and wealthy life in every sense of the word. Happy, spirit filled, at peace and fulfilled.

The star of my own show. The leading lady. In pursuit of excellence. A story that is not defined by societal limitations. A story that is in conformity with God's will. A beautiful story inside out. A story where am blessed. Am highly favored, loved and appreciated. A story where am connected to a healthy and loving community. A story where am of service and making a contribution to society. A story where I have a vision, mission, clearly defined values and a roadmap.

That said, am inspired by Confucius quote, "our greatest glory is not in never falling but in rising every time we fall". I dust myself up and interrogate further.

What got me stuck? What may have contributed to not living my ideal story? What is God's Will for my life?

Truth be told, other than a series of bad choices, lack of guidance, ignorance and naivety mentioned, a lack of focus on what is important may have led to my current situation. Allowing myself to be distracted by the environment. More in tune with the outside in, as opposed to the inside out. Allowing myself to be influenced by the outside as opposed to influencing what is on the outside. Allowing things to happen as opposed to making things happen. Not being intentional and deliberate in my day to day living. For the most part, not setting my own agenda thus setting myself up to being vulnerable to other people's agenda.

The offenses we carry along also compound the situation of being stuck, the never ending scripts in our quest to live out the life's chronos. We end up carrying around a lot of issues, commonly referred to as garbage, which conforms to all rules of gravity. As we cannot soar while carrying tons of garbage. We are also stuck due to our self-defeating life patterns and or belief patterns.

This is further compounded by the little knowledge and encounter with God, His purpose and will for our lives. A lack of vision. A lack of spelt out SMART goals and a lack of discipline. It therefore follows, that there is need to read scripture for ourselves, know God and experience God in our every day life.

In addition, the situation is aggravated by a lack of self-awareness. Not knowing who we are. Resulting in identity issues. This is made increasingly worse when we allow other people's opinions to affect and influence our thoughts and actions as we may fail to recognize our own value outside the societal opinions, thus often selling ourselves short.

Leaning on the validation of others, is often a major drawback. In most cases, it leads one to getting involved in toxic relationships and associations in pursuit of validation, which eventually drain the life out of us.

Furthermore, in our quest to fit in, desire to belong and find social validation, we often lose our authentic self. This is made worse by the urge to connect and identify with a group while not being deliberate and thoughtful of the value system of the groups we seek and engage in. As a result, we end up in the wrong company, which may increasingly lead one to warped belief systems, corrupt thinking and or negative influences.

We may also encounter people who want to have control over us, bring us down, bring our self-esteem down, rob us off our joy, serenity and security. Often resulting in a low emotional state. Many a time, left reeling in a sense of insecurity, unworthiness, inadequacy and of not being capable.

Noteworthy, is that the society is full of the so called haters and critics, who more often than not, yield power and influence. Their modus operandi being that of character assassination, manipulation, betrayal, guilt tripping and lies to serve their selfish interests, motives, desires and or to take control.

Social media may also propel one to the proverbial rat race as we try to measure up to the societal and or social media standards. Always comparing, competing and living out the rat race with other members of the community on matters beauty, mental, professional, social, cultural, spiritual and financial standing. Wanting to please and live out the societal flashy imagery thus putting on a lot of pressure on ourselves.

Moreover, one may be overly stuck due to their wounded self, especially in situations where one has experienced physical and or emotional abuse.

One may be carrying along a lot of baggage, trauma, pain, brokenness, wounded self, hurts, stigma, mental turmoil, spiritual conflict, anger and resentment. This results in emotional issues which then begin to affect a person's thinking and handling of health, physical appearance, work, social relations, spiritual matters and or financial resources.

Wanting to prove ourselves worthy, we may seek vengeance and or try to vindicate ourselves in varied ways and or extremes. For others, we witness, overwhelming self-expression. That is, how one identifies and expresses themselves.

Inadvertently, for others, they seek out negative coping mechanisms, evidenced in addictions, procrastination, excuses, negative attitude, denial, fight, flight, avoidance and or hostility to best deal with their inner struggles.

Noteworthy, is that for the vast majority, the wounded self may inherently be as a result of childhood abuse. The resulting trauma may be worse. As the inner child may have faced traumatic events, experiences and or circumstance with resultant deep emotional scars, wounds and pain with no sense of relief, way out and or exit plan. A feeling of being imprisoned since they had little or no control over their environment.

The child facing abuse suffers from being overly helpless and in most cases with no one to assist them process their ravaging emotions. This results in unprocessed childhood trauma that manifests throughout life including adulthood.

Consciously or unconsciously, the now adult, lives out and acts out on the basis of past issues. A soul that is battling with low self-worth. Furthermore, consciously and or unconsciously searching for love, acceptance and understanding.

In the midst of the turmoil, what we witness are persons who for the most part are seeking out unqualified relationships, spaces and substances to nurse their emotional wounds and pain.

This may present itself in a consistent downward spiraling, inconsistent state, warped thoughts, negative responses, extreme actions, attitudes, irrational behavior, unexplained habits and or fire-fighting mode of the now adult.

Understandably, their character may be due to a weak spirit and the battle in the mind. For the mind bears within itself a myriad of subconscious memories and emotions. The trauma leads one to constantly being susceptible to feelings of being lost, being confused, unworthy, inadequate, incapable, lacking in self-confidence and being insecure.

For others, the spirit of fear may also creep in. Particularly if you have little or no spiritual knowledge. A lack of faith. Lack of faith in God, self and society. Not to mention the difficulty to forgive and reconcile with the past and or present traumatic events.

The victim continually making negative confessions, cursing, seeking vengeance and vindication, which then becomes a stumbling block for God's grace and blessings. What follows is that one becomes their own worst enemy. Standing in the way of their own blessed destiny.

And when the wilderness does present itself, it is easy to fall by the wayside. For the wilderness experience is said to be a make or break season in our lives. A disruption to our comfort zone.

Many may not understand what is happening. The shaking. The clamoring. The test and the awakening. Many may not understand that God in His love and compassion, is on a mission to reboot, reset and restart their lives. His own way of developing the character. Renewing of the mind. Directing one to a paradigm shift as one would want to call it. A humbling experience.

Where one is called upon, to not lean on their own understanding. To surrender to God, trust and obey. To remain still. To seek out God's purpose and will for their lives.

One can only imagine how profound it must have been for Peter to have to witness Jesus calming the storm and or the time Jesus called on him to walk on water.

It therefore follows that given all the noise around us, discomfort and lack of knowledge, we miss out on what God is doing and constantly find ourselves battling with the external and asking God, "where are you" instead of "why" and "what should I learn" from the season.

Struggling to remain still. Refusing to surrender to God and instead seeking out someone and or something to rescue us and love us. Someone and or something that will bring happiness and comfort to our lives.

In the meantime, idolatry may also set in as we seek out people and or substances that will offer escape from the disturbing circumstances that we find ourselves in, while in pursuit of meaning, love, acceptance, security, consolation, happiness, comfort and validation.

Only grace can save our poor souls. For the downward spiral, chips into our very core. Our spiritual lives. Threatening to separate us from God, His blessings and love.

It is at this time that Hosea 4:6 rings so true. As it is said that God's people are destroyed for lack of knowledge. A lack of wisdom. It is no wonder that Jesus on the cross interceded on behalf of man, as inscribed in Luke 23:34, "Father, forgive them, for they do not know what they are doing".

God is said to be good all the time. God is not malicious. God is compassionate. In his mercy, unmerited favor and patience offers us an opportunity for a turnaround. For redirection. For healing. For His unconditional love and grace. The ball is in our court, to accept or reject Him.

I choose to follow God. I choose to surrender to God. For a turnaround. Albeit with little strength left. So begins a journey. An attempt to rewrite my story. To revisit my script. Hopefully anchored on the word and the will of God. Fully surrendered. Taking into account that I am a work in progress. On a journey to sanctification and salvation. A journey on God's narrow path. A journey inspired by God's promises. A journey of hope. A journey where I can in the end confess that I have fought the good fight, finished the race and kept the faith.

It is never too late nor too early to take that route. The journey is not easy though and must come from an appreciation that God has good plans for us, plans for prosperity and not disaster, plans for the future that we hope for as Jeremiah aptly puts it in Jeremiah 29:11. Also, that only God knows my tomorrow, for He is the Alpha and Omega. God knit me and has a plan and purpose for my life.

Moreover, whatever plan there is, only God can make it happen. For with God, all things are possible as declared in Mathew 11:30.

Jesus urges us on. To lean on Him, "For my yoke is easy and burden is light" and to take comfort that He is the Way, the Truth and the life and in Him we are more than conquerors.

Assessing the instruments

So begins a journey to rewrite my story while pondering on how one is supposed to summon the strength and energy to rise from a perceived fall? How does one keep moving, day in, day out when all semblance of normalcy has been wiped out from underneath you? All my adult years, I had grown accustomed to having a business, a furnished house and a car. My comfort zone.

I recollect, all was well until the enemy came knocking. Like Eve, may have knowingly and or unknowingly opened the door to the enemy who is always lurking in wait for the prey. As the good book says, in John 10:10, the enemy comes only to steal, kill and destroy. What followed was a series of events leading to the not so pleasant outcomes as evidenced in my present circumstances where instead of having to sit in my ideal office and or furnished living room, I am in a living room cum office with only a working table and an office chair.

I hold on to the promise as written in Romans 8:28 that everything works out for the good of those who love the Lord. I want to believe that God will use the opportunity that the enemy set to destroy me to redirect me. My prayer being for God's help to discern the season.

That said, days on end, I keep at the grind, my external circumstances notwithstanding. In fact, constantly reminding me that all is not well. Days when anxiety creeps in as I wonder if at all I will see the light of day.

If and when, I will have a semblance of normalcy or should I resign to my new normal? I ponder. All the while holding on to every ounce of hope still left whereas the world around gleefully highlighting and spelling out my fate. Condemning me and throwing all manner of jibes. I could totally relate with a number of characters in the bible who struggled with disruption in their lives and battle with God's promises.

What keeps me going however is the constant meditation which is often interjected by the questioning, murmuring and complaining to God for the narrative that has set over my life. Not that the murmuring helps.

Living in constant fear and despair. Knowing only too well that questioning, complaining and murmuring will not work in my favor. In fact, may result in separation from God and or dire consequences. Quite the reverse of what I hope for.

I can relate with Jacob. The wrestle is real. I can also relate with Job. Fighting with the Word. Wrestling to keep up the hope and belief that in the fullness of time, I will see God's glory. That as they say, dawn is nigh. And to hold on to the belief that it is usually darkest before dawn.

I recall my bible study lessons where the Word reiterated steadfast faith, to trust and obey. To be still and to know that He is God.

Naturally, I want microwave answers to my endless string of prayers. Why the wait, Oh my Lord, King of Kings? On the other hand, am reminded that His ways are truly not our ways. All I can do is try and summon all strength with each passing day. Praying for grace and faith to endure yet another grueling day as I grapple through the darkness not knowing as and when the light would shine through. When I would finally see the proverbial end of the dark tunnel.

In those dark moments, I find that the best option is to keep the gratitude up, as hard as it is. To try and reconcile with the facts of my given circumstances. To be still. To remain hopeful. For this is indeed darkness and by no means a comfort zone.

The silver lining to the wilderness experience, hopefully, is that over time one surrenders to God and not to the wills of the world. One accepts that God's ways, are not our ways.

What follows is transformation. A bitter sweet moment. A moment where the self-succumbs to the will of God. The moment when we realize that we are called not just for ourselves but for the greater good of society and will of God.

It is often said that transformation happens when we are crushed, under pressure and in darkness. Again, by no means in the comfort zone. The popular saying being that, grapes are crushed to make wine, diamonds are formed under pressure, olives are pressed to produce olive oil and seeds are planted in the dark soil, thus, similarly we go through challenging times to bring out the best in us.

And as the Psalmist wrote in 51:17, "A broken spirit, a broken and contrite heart, O God, you will not despise". The same is reiterated in Psalm 34:18, "The Lord is near to the broken hearted and saves the crushed in spirit". Thus, the challenging times may also be orchestrated to bring us closer to God and or appreciate His being in our lives.

For as Paul wrote in 2nd Corinthians 12:9 "And He said unto me, my grace is sufficient for thee, for my strength is made perfect in weakness. Most gladly therefore will I rather glory in my infirmities that the power of Christ may rest upon me". It therefore goes to show that that we are sustained by grace and this becomes even more apparent in our weakest times.

It is no wonder that the Word reiterates that it is only at the breaking of the bread by Jesus, did the disciples who had walked with him to Emmaus have an awakening that their companion had been Jesus. For the disciples knew of Jesus, all the while, on their way to Emmaus but the disciples did not recognize Jesus. The disciples were not consciously aware that they were walking with Jesus in spite of their hearts burning from within. Only in retrospect, following the breaking of the bread, did they acknowledge that they had indeed been walking the journey with Jesus Christ all the while.

Similarly, it is only while journeying through the desert experience and are broken, do we fully appreciate His grace, fully surrender to the events of the day and the will of God. Like fragile clay jars containing this great treasure, the treasure is revealed to demonstrate that there is greater power within us and that the power in us is from God, not of ourselves. That though broken-hearted and crushed in spirit, God is very close and dear.

This may not be self-evident through our normal day to day lives, surrounded by the noise, the rat race and or comfort zones, where we lean into our own strength, wisdom, knowledge, resources and or networks.

Again Paul, in 2nd Corinthians 4, urges us on, that though "We are pressed on every side by troubles, but we are not crushed. We are perplexed, but not driven to despair. We are hunted down, but never abandoned by God. We get knocked down, but we are not destroyed. Through suffering, our bodies continue to share in the death of Jesus so that the life of Jesus may also be seen in our bodies. We live under constant danger of death because we serve Jesus, so that the life of Jesus will be evident in our dying bodies. So we live in the face of death, but this has resulted in eternal life for you".

In addition, in verse 16-18, we are encouraged to remain in faith, "never give up. Though our bodies are dying, our spirits are being renewed every day. For our present troubles are small and won't last very long. Yet they produce for us a glory that vastly outweighs them and will last forever." So we are encouraged not to look at the troubles we can see now, rather, to fix our gaze on things that cannot be seen. For the things we see now will soon be gone, but the things we cannot see will last forever.

As often said and witnessed, the Christian walk is not devoid of challenges. Paul confessed, in 2 Corinthians 12:7-8 "in order to keep me from becoming conceited, I was given a thorn in my flesh, a messenger of Satan, to torment me. Three times I pleaded with the Lord to take it away from me".

A thorn in the flesh may be something given to us by God to keep us from becoming conceited. It will make us feel uncomfortable, tormented, tortured. However, God does not torture his children. His help can come in the form of discipline and trials, but His purpose is always to strengthen us, challenge us to put our trust in Him and to conform us into the image of Christ.

It is also in crisis that character is revealed. All claim to be Christians. All waiting for Christ's appearing. But crisis reveals the true character of man. As Jesus said at the end of the Sermon on the Mount, Luke 6:48, the wise man hears the word, digs down deep and builds his house on a rock. The foolish man hears it, but he doesn't dig down, he builds superficially on the sand. Then when the storm hits, it is the wise man's house that stands firm.

The same is reiterated in Mathew 13:23 where Jesus in the parable talks of "the one who received the seed that fell on good soil is the man who hears the word and understands it. He produces a crop, yielding a hundred, sixty or thirty times what was sown".

Mathew 7 emphasizes that "A good tree cannot bring forth evil fruit, neither can a corrupt tree bring forth good fruit. Wherefore by their fruits ye shall know them".

Authentic Christians are revealed in times of crisis and by their fruit. Like the parable of the ten virgins, five are found not ready. It is therefore critical to have a solid spiritual belief system and oneness with God to withstand the storm.

As much as life happens and as difficult as it is to process the pain, we are reminded in Romans 5:3-5 that "glory in our sufferings, because we know that suffering produces perseverance; perseverance, character and character, hope. And hope does not put us to shame, because God's love has been poured out into our hearts through the Holy Spirit, who has been given to us".

Moreover, it is believed that poor attitude is a manifestation of poor character. Good character commands respect. When character is lacking and or seemingly lost. One may also have a poor reputation and low morale. Thus the need to appreciate crisis for the likely added benefit of developing character, self-worth and command respect.

Furthermore, one comes to the realization in retrospect that despite the character development during the crisis, there is a blessing attached to it, if one looks hard enough.

As the 35th US president, John F. Kennedy succinctly put it "When written in Chinese, the word 'crisis' is composed of two characters. One represents danger and the other represents opportunity".

In hindsight, I would say, the desert experience has provided me an opportunity to not only meditate on God's word, but also to live out God's word. In addition, the isolation, gave me an opportunity to review the lessons learnt in bible study and to hold fast to God's word which helped to chart the way forward.

As they say, a journey of a thousand miles starts with the first step. The journey inward is by no means a short journey. A journey where one is always in constant reflection, depending on the season. A journey where one is in constant introspection in relation to their respective purpose and mission. The key being to remain focused and on course in the midst of all the noise.

Mending the sails

It is widely believed that one cannot repeatedly do the same thing and expect different results. That the expectation of different results would border insanity.

Hence the need to establish the cause and effect to my current situation. To revisit my belief system, what is my belief system, why do I believe what I believe and why do I act the way I do? As Proverbs 23 verse 7 so aptly puts it "As a man thinketh in his heart, so is he".

What do I believe of myself and the world around me? For as mentioned, most if not all of us struggle with self-identity and low self-esteem. May explain the self-doubt and lack of confidence.

It is not uncommon. Even in biblical times, we encounter the likes of Gideon and Moses who when called upon to do the will of God were hesitant due to their perceived inability for the task ahead.

A prime example would be Moses. Moses was hesitant to take up the calling by God. And when push came to shove, Moses asked God whom he should say had sent him. Seemingly to redirect the attention from himself. And God replied to Moses, "I AM WHO I AM". This is what you are to say to the Israelites: I AM has sent me to you". Thus Moses leaned on who God was as opposed to who he was or what he perceived himself to be, as he evidently did not find himself worthy. Often questioning God as to his ability to deliver His will.

Not surprising, we are also faced with the same self-doubt as there are many voices in our mind and around us, that wage war against our true identity in Christ. Our mistakes, struggles, experiences, embarrassing moments and negative thoughts for instance, blur our identity in Christ. The battle is for the most part within. That is, battle in the mind.

Conflicted in thought due to our own shortfalls, thoughts of not being able, not being worthy, not enough, not loveable, a misfit, misunderstood, labeled and or not acceptable. God, on the other hand, constantly reminding us that we are unconditionally loved and accepted. That we are fearfully and wonderfully made. We are well equipped for the calling.

In addition, *God reminds us that we are righteous before Him, for we were redeemed, when He gave up His only son to die for our sin. That we are reconciled to Himself. Hence, by grace, we are God's children. That we are loved, found worthy, accepted and capable in Jesus Christ. That we are not of our own and certainly not of the world. That the world should not define us, but instead, we should be defined by God. That we are priceless and like Jesus on earth, on a divine mission and assignment.*

The Word also urges us to guard our hearts. Which means protecting ourselves from things that would harm us including our thoughts. We have to overcome the thoughts that are not in conformity with the Word of God.

To find ways to overcome doubts that tend to creep in and compromise our faith. To recognize and acknowledge that Satan the accuser has a way of creeping into our thoughts as witnessed in Zechariah 3 where Joshua is standing before the Angel of the LORD and Satan is standing at his right hand to accuse Joshua. And the LORD says to Satan, "The LORD rebuke you, Satan! The LORD who has chosen Jerusalem rebuke you! Is this not a brand, Joshua, plucked from the fire?".

It is therefore, only fair to interrogate our thought patterns as Satan is always at hand to accuse, judge and condemn us. Beware, Satan the liar is consistently fighting believers to cause us to lose sight of our true identity and belonging. To separate us from God. To separate us from our heritage.

God on the other hand is consistently pouring out His grace and reminding us of who we are in Christ Jesus. That we were redeemed and made righteous in Christ Jesus. God is constantly reminding us not to dwell on our failures like the prodigal son, but to receive His grace and remain focused on Him.

It is with this realization that am inclined to revisit my thought patterns. What patterns are evident in my thinking, spoken word, actions and or inaction? Have my thought patterns contributed to my current situation? What do I need to change?

To quote a famous saying by Lao Tzu is to "Watch your thoughts, they become your words; watch your words, they become your actions; watch your actions, they become your habits; watch your habits, they become your character; watch your character, it becomes your destiny."

Further, in Philippians 4: 8 we are urged, "brothers and sisters, whatever is true, whatever is noble, whatever is right, whatever is pure, whatever is lovely, whatever is admirable, if anything is excellent or praiseworthy, think about such things".

It is said that our thoughts, our ideas, opinions and beliefs about ourselves and the world around us inform our reaction and or response to any situation or experience as they influence our bias, action and or inaction.

Noteworthy, an attitude, is said to be a manifestation of a long held thought, which develops from thoughts, to the words we speak, actions and or habits, which are then repeated over and reinforced in the mind.

It is generally held that our thoughts are shaped by our life experiences, socialization, culture, associations, environment and or education.

That said, if one is aware of their thoughts and attitudes, one can revisit and choose to change their negative thought patterns.

The challenge for most though, is that one's thought process may be so ingrained and or one may not be consciously aware thus difficult to change overnight.

This is especially the case where one has a negative and or poor attitude which may be due to challenging, distressful and arguably unfair life experiences over time. Thoughts and belief systems thereof become heavily skewed. Hence, what becomes quite apparent over time is the negative thought patterns, attitudes, emotional and or physical reactions to various life situations.

Fortunately, and or unfortunately, no one escapes some kind of tragedy in life. In fact, John 16:33 states that, we shall face tribulation in the world. On the other hand, the Psalmist in 14:3, comforts us with the knowledge that God heals the broken hearted and binds up their wounds. That when we hold onto our faith, God becomes our strength, our healer, our comforter and our counsellor. He understands our pain, as He has suffered Himself for our sins.

One may even be experiencing the challenge at present, day in day out with no sign of relief. This results in being anxious, discouraged and stressed. James 5:13 urges us to pray whenever we find ourselves afflicted and enduring hardship. In Psalm 13, David prayed and lamented such, "How long, Lord? Will you forget me forever? How long will you hide your face from me? How long must I wrestle with my thoughts, day after day, have sorrow in my heart? How long will my enemy triumph over me? Look on me and answer, Lord my God. Give light to my eyes, or I will sleep in death, and my enemy will say, I have overcome him and my foes will rejoice when I fall. But I trust in your unfailing love. My heart rejoices in your salvation. I will sing the Lord's praise, for he has been good to me".

Obviously David was in distress. He was however authentic before God, of his pain, asking God to remember him and to come to his rescue. David recounted God's character, of His unfailing love and salvation. David trusted God. Thus he did not hesitate to sing praises to His Lord even in his distress, knowing only too well that in the fullness of time, he would be saved.

Granted, one may not feel like trusting God. Particularly if one has been through situations and or circumstances that did not go as hoped. What follows naturally, is doubt begins to set in.

Despite the situation and or circumstances, *Isaiah 55:8 reminds us that "For my thoughts are not your thoughts, neither are your ways my ways, declares the Lord. For as the heavens are higher than the earth, so are my ways higher than your ways, and my thoughts higher than your thoughts".*

Further, in Proverbs 19:21, we are reminded that "Many are the plans in a person's heart, but it is the Lord's purpose that prevails". In God's wisdom and grace, events may not always churn out as we had hoped.

That notwithstanding, we remain hopeful. Ultimately, it is our choice. A choice to trust God. An act of the will. To trust that we will indeed find healing, restoration and salvation. A choice to invite God for spiritual healing and reconciliation with God.

Healing is said to be arguably a lifelong process which we experience through the grace of God, faith in Jesus Christ and the power of the Holy Spirit. To forgive self and others for words spoken, words not said, action and or inaction which may have been offensive to say the least.

Healing brings the love of God within us and the power of the Holy spirit. We also end up manifesting the fruit of the Holy Spirit, which is love, joy, peace, longsuffering, kindness, goodness and faithfulness as spelt out in Galatians 5:22.

Recovery

It makes little or no sense in filling water into broken jars. On the same token, it is argued that God will not pour His blessings into broken vessels thus the need for healing.

Healing then enables one to proactively and effectively deal with the different facets of life such as one's mental state, psychological state, financial matters, physical health, social relations and spiritual matters.

To find healing, it is recommended one be honest with themselves. To confront where you have been, what happened or is happening. This may involve answering some tough questions such as do I carry baggage? Are there people I hate or blame for issues within or without? Who is my enemy, abuser and or my goliath? What is the elephant in the room? When did the hate or offense begin? Who is to blame? Who and or what initiated the hate or offense? What did the offender do or not do, say or did not say?

That said, to receive healing one has to end the blame game and own the process. It is said that finger pointing or blaming others is an outward manifestation of the root of bitterness. Resentment if you like. When we prefer to blame others for all the wrong in us and not taking personal responsibility for the hate, resentment and unforgiveness built up inside, which holds us back from getting healed.

One may even associate their pain and or hurt with God. Are you blaming God? The word tells us that God is not the source of our problems. Our sin separates us from God. Also, blaming God for our problems will not resolve the problem. We need to make peace with God so as to experience God's healing in our mind and emotions.

In 2 Timothy 1:7, God states that a sound mind comes from knowing Him. Meaning that only He can save and deliver us from spiritual death. Thus, instead of turning away from God as the enemy would want, to draw closer to Him. As only

God can revive, resuscitate and breathe life into our spirits. Jesus reiterates this by calling on all those who are heavy laden in Matthew 11: 28-29, including those who are carrying emotional baggage, to come to Him and He will give them rest.

In any case we are reminded in Isaiah 53:4 that "Surely he hath borne our griefs and carried our sorrows, grief, pain, affliction, yet we did esteem him stricken, smitten of God, and afflicted. But he was wounded for our transgressions, he was bruised for our iniquities, the chastisement of our peace was upon him and with his stripes we are healed".

That does not sound like a person who is malicious and or intends harm. To the contrary, *God has good intentions for us. Again, Jeremiah 29:11 affirms that, "For I know the thoughts that I think toward you, saith the Lord, thoughts of peace and not of evil, to give you an expected end".* Whereas John 11:35-36 tells us that Jesus wept on seeing the people in distress. Further in John 3:16, it is said that God so loved the world that He allowed the crucifixion of His beloved son as an atonement for our sins yet He had earlier spared Abraham the agony of sacrificing his beloved son Isaac. This only goes to show His unconditional love for man.

On the flip side, the issue could be something that one regrets doing. To find healing, it is recommended that one approaches God at His seat of mercy. To address any feelings of guilt, shame and in particular feelings that God may be disappointed or angry. For God loves, forgives and accepts each person without exception. It is said that He redeemed us while we were still sinners. How much more when we choose to be reconciled to Him?

In Psalm 55:22, He urges us "Cast your burden on the Lord, and he will sustain you, he will never permit the righteous to be moved". Further, in 1st Peter 5:7, God's word tells us to cast our cares upon Him, for He cares for us. That is, to turn our burdens over to Jesus and trust Him to take care of them.

The key, is to completely surrender ourselves. Not in part. For when we do not let down our burden of shame, we hinder the inner healing process.

In essence, when we do not fully surrender, it is seen as a manifestation of one's denial of the grace we receive from Jesus Christ.

Thus the need to settle it in our minds that God is not angry with us. To believe in God's Word about our sins being forgiven. To forgive ourselves, accept the love and grace extended to us by Jesus Christ.

It is also vital that we see ourselves as God sees us, cleansed and made righteous through the blood of Jesus. Not to continue beating ourselves up as if you haven't been forgiven. To shed off the guilt and condemnation. To come to a realization that our sins were forgiven at the cross.

We are also encouraged to sincerely confess our sin and pain as it is believed that transparency is important for the healing process of emotional wounds.

It is also often said that once a problem or issue is shared, the problem may be half solved. Hence, one may also consider sharing their pain and or struggle with a spiritual leader who may intercede on their behalf.

An Intercessory prayer, if you may. This is proclaimed in James 5:16, that "the effectual fervent prayer of a righteous man availeth much". The same is witnessed in the bible verse where Job interceded on behalf of his friends as guided by God. Moses also interceded on behalf of the Israelites on several occasions, resulting in God turning away His intended anger and wrath on the people.

In addition, we are encouraged to be thankful throughout the healing process, as it is said that an unthankful heart is prone to being unforgiving, unloving, resentful and having hateful feelings against others. Also, an unthankful heart is like poison to our emotional health and hinders the healing that God wants to bring to our hearts and minds.

To forgive. Often, those who are unforgiving and judgmental towards others, forget what God has done for them. It goes without saying that anyone who is truly thankful for God's mercies will extend the same compassion and mercy to others.

Another key to inner healing is not to overthink what was done and or what may have happened. To consciously make an effort to think of pure thoughts and focus on Jesus Christ. To focus on the cross.

Understandably it is easier said than done and hence the need to pray for God's grace so as to remain focused on the cross. To receive healing and enlightenment.

Paramount, is one's commitment to resolving the problem and not to dwell on the problem. Commitment to finding a solution. Meditating on the solution with the aim of experiencing inner healing and forging ahead. To be on the watch of their thought patterns, not to wallow in negative feelings that could lead to a deadly spell of depression, when reminded of all the wrong and injustice and or the temptation to seek vengeance.

To let go and let God. Not to give in to the feelings of hate and resentment. To take solace in Deuteronomy 32:35 where God assures us that "Vengeance is Mine, and recompense, their foot shall slip in due time, for the day of their calamity is at hand, and the things to come hasten upon them".

Moreover, in the Lord's prayer, Jesus made it clear that if we want to be forgiven, we have to forgive others. That we need to forgive others and extend the same mercy and forgiveness that we seek from God.

The parable of the unforgiving servant best illustrates this in Mathew 18:21-35. The parable tells the story of a king who was calling in debts from his servants. One servant owed a huge amount of money which he could not pay. The king ordered that the man and his family be sold into slavery to pay off the debt. The man pleaded for mercy and begged for more time. The king decided to have compassion on him and wrote off the debt. As fate would have it, this same servant was owed a relatively smaller amount by another servant. Ironically, even after being granted mercy by the king for a larger debt, the unforgiving servant demanded that his colleague pay his debt. When the fellow servant was unable to pay, the unforgiving servant sent him to prison until he paid. When the incident was reported to the king that the forgiven servant refused to forgive, the king went ahead to renounce his mercy from the man and sent him to prison until his debt was paid. Jesus concludes by saying that God like the king, is willing to show mercy and forgiveness to those that are also forgiving and merciful to others.

Granted, our feelings of pain, hurt, anger, resentment are legitimate and valid. However, our unforgiving and hardened hearts form a stumbling block for not receiving healing, blessings and forging a relationship with God.

Further, it is our own reactions to what was done to us which holds us ransom. Our own anger, hate, resentment and unforgiveness, which keeps us in a spiritual prison.

Noteworthy, is that in as much as we may not be responsible for what happened or is happening to us, we are however responsible for how we choose to react and or respond to the hurt, pain and or situation we may find ourselves in.

It is recommended therefore to try and remain calm, process the emotion following an event and choose to make a positive step forward. Keeping in mind that it is not what was done to us that keeps us in bondage, but our reaction to what was done to us which will determine if we remain in spiritual bondage and torment.

In forgiving others, we not only allow healing but also live in obedience to the commandment given by Jesus in John 15:12, "This is my commandment, that ye love one another, as I have loved you", keeping in mind that when we allow resentment and unforgiveness to reign in our hearts, we are disobeying the commandment which works to our disadvantage as the sin separates us from God.

Charting the course

Having been through the refinery and working my way to healing, I begin to ponder, what next?

Does one go back to the old script? Am I happy with the old script? Do I want to rewrite the script? And taking into account that God gives me free will to make choices, what is the best course of action?

Does one put new wine into old wine skin? Will it be about carrying around baggage? Have I shed the baggage? Will it be about a self-serving agenda? Will it be about me, myself and I? Will it be all about mammon and satisfying the ego? Will it be about fulfilling the societal agenda and riding the never ending rat race and roller coaster?

On the other hand, will it be about purpose, new mindset, new attitude, positive value system, peace, love, joy, finding the true north, being centered in Christ, fulfilling God's will, bearing fruit, adding value, alleviating pain in society? Will it be about serving? Will it be about living a passionate, abundant and fulfilled life? Will it be about living life on my own terms, without societal pressure? Will it be about living life in alignment to the spirit? Will it be aligned to a desired eternal life?

How does one begin to rewrite their own script? Is it even possible?

In Proverbs 16:9, the bible tells us that we may make our plans but God has the last word. The same is emphasized by Jesus as written in Luke 12:16-2, when he gave the parable, "the ground of a certain rich man yielded an abundant harvest. He thought to himself, what shall I do? I have no place to store my crops. Then he said, this is what I will do. I will tear down my barns and build bigger ones, and there I will store my surplus grain. And I will say to myself, you have plenty of grain laid up for many years. Take life easy, eat, drink and be merry. But God said to him, you fool! This very night your life will be demanded from you.

Then who will get what you have prepared for yourself? This is how it will be with whoever stores up things for themselves but is not rich toward God."

We can therefore safely conclude that the script can only bear fruit if God endorses it. And as Amos 3:3 put it, "Can two walk together, except they be agreed?"

The foregoing reaffirms the need to be reconciled to God and his purpose for our lives. To seek Him first, for His leading. In turn, He will meet our heart's desires. That is, our hopes, dreams and work plans. After all, He is God, the all-knowing and powerful God. The Alpha and Omega. He knows our beginning from the end. Therefore, God would be best suited to guide us on the way forward.

Needless to say, God is our potter. He has a purpose for us on earth. To bear fruit. Each to their own intended purpose as it is said, our respective purpose is as unique as our individual fingerprints.

Notably, we all have unique talents, experiences, skill sets and interests. And as Albert Einstein once said, *"The meaning of life is to discover our gifts. The purpose of life is to give them away."*

The primary assignment in life would then be in finding and writing our purpose. To have an appreciation and an awareness of our purpose on earth.

Noteworthy, purpose is the long run. There could be a different purpose in every season of a person's life.

To begin with, how does one identify if they are on the right path to fulfilling their intended purpose? Some may already know their unique talents and passions whereas others may simply be going through life. Not knowing or aware of their unique talents as they seem so ordinary.

The Japanese are said to offer a concept known as ikigai that helps one to identify their purpose. The concept subscribes to one identifying facets of their lives that seem easy, gives them intrinsic authentic peace, love, joy and passion.

The ikigai concept is also said to be about finding the overlap between what one loves doing and what the world needs, with what you are good at and what the world will pay for.

It is about pursuing your passions while meeting the needs of the world around us.

I choose to subscribe to the said concept, in the hope that it will help bring clarity to my intended purpose and will of God in my life.

Foremost, the Ikigai concept requires one to explore what one loves. That is, to note down the things you love in life that bring you joy. This may be informed by my dreams, desires, passion, interests, experiences, talents, skills, environment, personalities and or role models.

Secondly, explore what am good at. That is, the things that am talented in, good and or skilled at. Also include what others may have spoken over me, complimented me on and or commented that am good at.

Third, explore what the world needs and matter to me. The things that the world needs which are in relation to my passion, skillset and talents.

Finally, explore what I can get paid for. That is, the things that I can get paid for which relate to my interests, passion, skillset and talents.

That done, I can then draw out my mission, vocation, profession and passion as illustrated.

That is, Mission being what I love, matters to me and the world needs. Vocation being what the world needs and I can also get paid for. Profession being what am good at and can get paid for. Whereas, passion being what I love and are also good at.

That which you love
That which you are good at
That which the world needs
That which you can be paid for
Passion
Mission
Profession
Vocation
Ikigai

The foregoing concept, not only helps me to identify my purpose but has also helped me to appreciate God's wiring in me. And just as machinery is made in conformity to its intended purpose, I realize, we are all gifted differently for our intended purpose.

Again, the gifts are intended not just for our own enjoyment but to be shared with others. As 1 Peter 4:10 emphasizes, "each of you should use whatever gift you have received to serve others as faithful stewards of God's grace".

The bible also reiterates in 1ˢᵗ Corinthians 16:14 that, "let all that you do, be done in love". Love in action. For God is love and we are made in His own image. Hence, it goes without saying that our intrinsic self only thrives in love.

Thus, in my quest to rewrite my desired script, to live a fulfilled and abundant life, am well aware of the need to remain authentic, to give and serve in love.

To ape the great, I AM and be a manifestation of love. To be Love. For we are, because of Love and are Love. We gain our being from Love. Hence the need for Love. We are always in pursuit of Love and seeking Love in action from those around us and from God.

Readjusting the sails

Foremost, it is recommended that I revisit my current status and or resources for the journey ahead.

In addition, to consider, if given the chance, what would be my perfect life. That is, how would it churn out? Given, all the money, support system, time, health and skillset, what would be my picturesque life be like? How is that compared to my current situation?

What needs to change? For as Mahatma Gandhi rightly put it "Be the change that you want to see in the world".

Likewise, what change do I want to see in my world?

Review	Ideal situation	Current situation	What needs to change
Health, nutrition, fitness, rest, environment, vacation, hobbies			
Intellect, education, skillset, self-improvement, career, vocation, mind-set			
Spiritual, wellness, belief system, faith, love, value system, habits, attitude, self-control, discipline			
Social interactions, relationships, parenting, networks, social media, image, behaviour, character, stereotyping, boundaries,			
Financial, income streams, budgeting, savings, investments, expenses			

Having reviewed some facets of my life, will attest that am not leading my desired life. I have some problem areas that need to be addressed.

All said and done; I may be faced with issues that are not within my control. Hence the need to extend myself grace and keep the serenity prayer in mind as I move along.

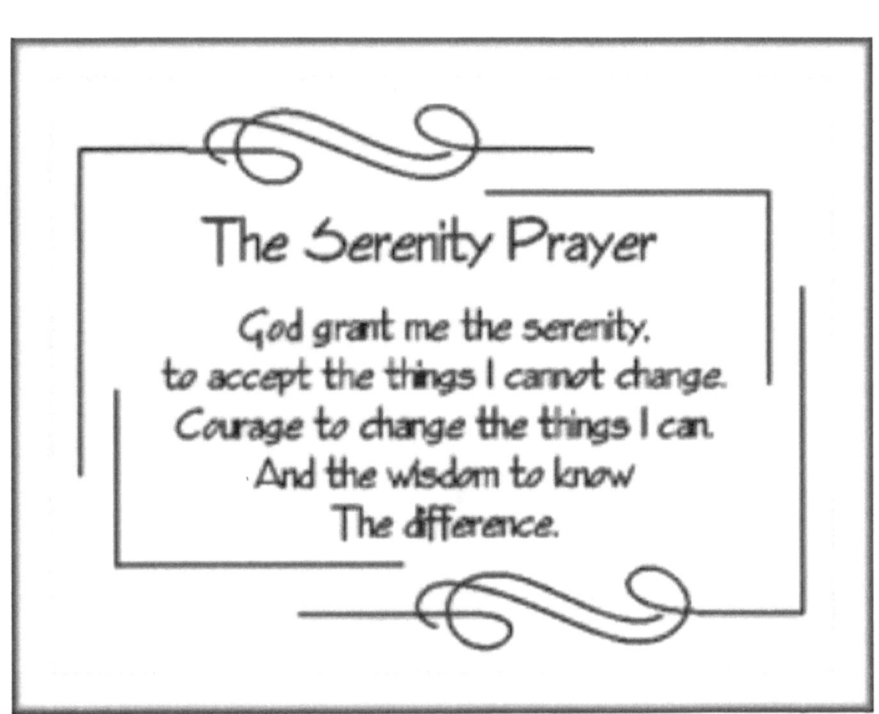

AND AS WE WORK OUT our desired lives, a word of caution, the ideals should not be heavily influenced by our inner wounds and trauma nor be influenced by societal expectations. Ideally be influenced by our authentic self, value system, passions, interests, persona, skillset, purpose and or vision.

We need to be consciously aware of inner wounds, trauma, self-limiting thought patterns, self-sabotaging patterns, habits and or behaviour that get in the way of leading our desired life.

A good place to start would probably be revisiting one's story and or life's journey. The good, the bad and the ugly.

Personal Exploration

Many wise men of old, have often said "Man know thyself; then thou shalt know the Universe and God".
It is with this foreknowledge that I can attempt to write my script.
Thus I begin to ponder.

- Who am I and where am I in my life's journey?

- Am I happy with my life story and or choices thus far? Am I guided by purpose, vision, mission, a plan and or goals?

- Do I have a well-articulated summary of my values, talents, passions, interests and skillset?

- Do I own my ideal story or has it been scripted for me by society?

- Do I own my life story or has it been scripted to match my family background, religion, tribe, culture, geographical location, gender, educational background, professional qualification, possessions, marital status, relationships, associations, social standing, business and or career?

- Is my current vocation and or profession a result of a well thought out plan and intention?

- If I had to rewrite my story, what would I write?

- What were the memorable moments of my life? The good, the bad and the ugly moments?

- How did the varied events and or experiences affect me?

- What positive and or negative feelings do I still carry along following the experiences?

- How did I respond to the respective events and or experiences?

- Of the negative experiences and or events, did I take time to process the joy, pain and or hurt? Did I respond positively and with love? Did I become better or bitter following the experiences and or events?

- What positive influence did the experiences have on me?

- Did the experiences ignite or hone strengths, interests, passions, skillsets and values that I was oblivious to?

- On the other hand, what negative influence did the experiences have on me?

- What belief systems, attitudes, mind-set, behaviour, patterns did I carry forward from the experiences?

- Based on the negative experiences, would I say I have unresolved drama, pain and hurt?

- Do I feel lost, rejected, neglected, betrayed, not seen, not heard, a burden and or do not matter?

- Did the negative experiences leave me with a sense of unworthiness, not enough, inadequate, incapable, insecure, not cared for, not loved, not accepted, disgraced, disrespected and or hopeless?

- How did the respective events and or experiences subsequently affect my thinking, subsequent action and or inaction?

- Did the respective events and or experiences affect my health, physical being, my appearance, self-esteem, my confidence, sense of security, work, career, business, spirit and or belief system?

- Also did the events and or experiences affect my decision making on matters finance and social interactions?

- Did the negative experiences lead me to seek out toxic relationships, negative associations, substance abuse, addictions or lifestyles that do not match my authentic self in an effort to find meaning, love, acceptance, security, consolation, happiness, comfort, validation, escape from inner wounds and or struggles.

- In addition, would I say the events and or experiences affected and or shaped my IDENTITY?

- Of the negative experiences and or events, whom do I need to Forgive?

- Do I need to forgive myself, parents, primary care givers, guardians, family, relatives, friends, teachers, colleagues, church leaders, church, and or leaders for what they said, did not say, their action and or inaction?

- Am I ready to consider that what they said, did not say, action and or inaction may have been borne from their own inner struggles, wounds, pain, hurt, brokenness, ignorance, lack of wisdom, misguided and or misinformation. Extending the same grace that our Lord Jesus Christ so richly gave us on the cross.

- On the flip side, can I identify with moments when I was not focused, was distracted, led by other people's agenda, carrying baggage, had trouble forgiving, living out societal expectations, struggling with stigma, blinded by bitterness/resentment, driven by peer pressure, having no spiritual guidance, having no meaning, lacking direction, no discipline, not self-aware, having identity issues, having no self-value, having no self-respect, desperate, depending on the validation of others, having toxic relationships, seeking belonging in wrong groups, not being authentic, not living up to my value system, allowing myself to be negatively influenced and or abused?

Personal frontier

Given the self-work and personal introspection thus far, who would I say I am? What is my intrinsic IDENTITY?

That is, moving past the societal expectations, opinions, labelling, criticism and or past mistakes, who would I say I am? Who would I say I am without the roles and or titles in my life? Who would God say I am? God is love. Am I love?

And as I mind map, where I have been and where I am at present, am reminded to keep in check any feelings of anger, bitterness and or resentment.

To bury the past hurts, to forgive, to let go and let God. To remember that God is not malicious. God may have allowed some experiences in order to reboot, reset and restart my life. Appreciate that it may be a wakeup call. A time to be more self-aware. A time to reclaim my true identity.

A time I am called upon to reflect and renew my mind. A time for a new mind-set. A time for a paradigm shift. A time to find my true north. A time to lean on God and not on my own understanding and or strength. A time to trust and obey God. A time to remain still and know God. A time to be centred and grounded in Jesus Christ. And a time to identify God's purpose for my life.

To appreciate that some events and or experiences may have been as a result of my bad choices, anger, resentment, bitterness, self-limiting belief systems, self-sabotaging life patterns, bad habits, bad behaviour, peer pressure, lack of focus, giving in to distractions, social media influence, fear, ignorance, naivety, emotional baggage, lack of motivation, lack of balance, lack of well-articulated values and or goals.

Moving forward, it is critical to be consciously aware of the issues that kept me away from achieving my optimum, thus becoming an impediment and stumbling block from achieving my ideal fulfilled & abundant life.

To constantly be aware of what keeps me stuck. To do the self-work, self-discovery and or self-improvement. To constantly interrogate my negative feelings, such as being unworthy, inadequate, incapable and or not enough that I may be susceptible to which affect my thinking and actions thereof.

To process the myriad of feelings and thoughts that overwhelm me. Also to keep in mind the famous saying by Lao Tzu, *"watch your thoughts, they become your words; watch your words, they become your actions; watch your actions, they become your habits; watch your habits, they become your character; watch your character, it becomes your destiny."*

And as Paul aptly put it in Philippians 4: 8, *"brothers and sisters, whatever is true, whatever is noble, whatever is right, whatever is pure, whatever is lovely, whatever is admirable, if anything is excellent or praiseworthy, think about such things"*.

To have steadfast faith and commitment to spiritual healing in order to remain on course. To continually seek out true love, acceptance, belonging, meaning and purpose in life, foremost from God.

To make peace with my past experiences which may in fact be stepping stones to revealing my identity, purpose and mission in life.

Thirdly, to articulate the values that I identify with, inspire me, relate with, make me happy, fulfilled, are important and or love doing? Also, identify the values would be best for the journey ahead? Such values include as under noted but not limited to;

Accomplishment

Accuracy

Acknowledgement

Adventure

Authenticity

Balance

Beauty

Boldness

Calm

Challenge

Collaboration

Community

Compassion

Comradeship

Confidence

Connectedness

Contentment

Contribution

Cooperation

Courage

Creativity

Curiosity

Determination

Directness

Discovery

Ease

Effortlessness

Empowerment

Enthusiasm

Environment

Excellence

Fairness

Flexibility

Focus

Forgiveness

Freedom

Friendship

Fun

Generosity

Gentleness

Growth

Happiness

Harmony

Health

Helpfulness

Honesty

Honour

Humour

Idealism

Independence

Innovation

Integrity

Intuition

Joy

Kindness

Learning

Listening

Love

Loyalty

Optimism

Orderliness

Participation

Partnership

Passion

Patience

Peace

Presence

Productivity

Recognition

Respect

Resourcefulness

Safety

Self-Esteem

Service

Simplicity

Spaciousness

Spirituality

Spontaneity

Strength

Tact

Thankfulness

Tolerance

Tradition

Trust

Truth

Understanding

Unity

Vitality

Wisdom

Further, given that that my respective duty and calling in life is as unique as my individual fingerprints, what would I say are my unique talents, skill-sets and interests that have shaped who I am? And how am I serving and or giving away my gifts?

With relation to my purpose and or calling, what life experiences, events, education and or vocation, may have revealed what I love in life, that bring me joy.

Further, which of my dreams, desires, passion, interests, talents, skills, environment, personalities and or role models inform my purpose in life.

What am I good at? What am I talented in, good and or skilled at. Also, what have others complimented me on and or commented that I am good at.

Given my world view, what does the world need and matters to me? Of the things that the world needs, which relate to my passion, skillset and talents.

In addition, what am I currently being paid for and or could potentially be paid to do? That is, the jobs that I can get paid for in relation to my experience, interests, passion, skillset and talents.

Having done the mind mapping, I can now delve deeper and draw out my respective mission, vocation, profession and passion based on the ikigai model.

<u>Mission</u>

Summary of <u>what do I love, matters to me</u> and the <u>what the world needs</u>

<u>Vocation</u>

Summary of <u>what does the world needs</u> and I can also <u>get paid for</u>

<u>Profession</u>

Summary of what I am <u>good at</u> and can <u>get paid for</u>

<u>Passion</u>

Summary of what I <u>love</u> and also <u>good at</u>

BASED ON MY SELF-ASSESSMENT, I can then chart out my respective purpose and mission.

That
which you
love
Passion
Mission
That
which
you are
good
at
Ikigai
That
which
the
world
needs
Profession
Vocation
That which
you can be
paid for

With the checklist done, I am hopefully at a place of self-awareness of my "Why". Why am here? What is my Mission?

A mission statement is said to hopefully entail a solution to a need. A solution to a people that require a service and or product that one is equipped and empowered to provide.

That said, the ikigai concept is not an end in itself, I must appreciate that I need to continually seek God's guidance and counsel.

In addition, I need to consistently revisit and review my life experiences, talents, skillsets, interests and passions in relation to situations and seasons in my life. Taking into account that different situations and or seasons may call on additional roles. That said, to make an effort to contribute and bear fruit on the journey, with love.

As the good book emphasizes in 1st Corinthians 16:14 that "let all that you do, be done in love". Love in action. God is love and everything He has done, is doing and will do, is done on the basis of unconditional love.

Similarly, I should be driven by love and service to the community. More so, as I am made in His own image, I would arguably be producing in my natural state, love personified.

Ultimately, striving to journey, live, learn and serve in love.

Dashboard

Moving forward, my take home, to recognise the importance of being self-aware and to own my identity. To be cognisant that society recognises me by my exterior such as by my name, photograph and or signature, which is just the tip of the iceberg while God identifies me by our calling.

In addition, to be aware that society has a tendency to identify one by their roles and or titles, the messaging by society however, tends to be shrouded with stereotyping.

To accept my authentic self. To identify and interrogate, where, what, how, from whom you get my identity, love, acceptance and or validation from. To be self-aware.

Notably, when one is self-aware, they are authentic. One can also easily articulate their experiences, likes, dislikes, passions, desires, goals, strengths, weaknesses, threats & opportunities, limitations, thought patterns, belief systems, culture and values.

In addition, one is aware of issues that affect their self-value and or identity such as insecurity issues, feelings of inadequacy, comparison, perfectionism, lack of confidence in self, impostor syndrome, criticism, inner critic, seeking approval from kitchen cabinet, past shortcomings, lack of skills and or resources, conforming to the ways of the world, not living up to society standards, social media conditioning and or socialisation.

Ideally, I should identify as love. In 1 John 4: 16, it is said that God is love. It follows then that if God is love and since I am said to be made in God's image, then I am indeed love. Love personified.

What is Love? 1 Corinthians 13:4-8, describes Love as "Love is patient, love is kind, love does not envy, is not boastful, is not arrogant, is not rude, is not self-seeking, is not irritable, and does not keep a record of wrongs, Love finds no joy in unrighteousness but rejoices in the truth. It bears all things, believes all things, hopes all things, endures all things. Love never ends."

To have an appreciation of character development over life's journey. To keep in mind that for the most part, character is developed in preparation for purpose. Acknowledging that God may take me on a journey to develop my character, for my intended purpose.

As mentioned, God is not malicious. To embrace the seasons set in preparation for the purpose. To comprehend that character development is critical in carrying out the assignment ahead. That is, equipping me to fulfil God's purpose and will. Prime examples in the good book include Joseph, Moses, David and Paul, whom God sent and prepared for the mission ahead.

Noting that character development may often be in the dark moments just like the seed in the soil or pictures in the dark room and may involve isolation and pressing times, where transformation does take place. The season may also be likened to the preparation of cut diamond, gold ornaments and or in the formation of a butterfly.

Thus, in order to remain afloat against the tide, to be anchored in Christ so as not to be shipwrecked. To be patient, hardworking, relentless, resilient and persistent throughout the journey. To be courageous, hopeful and teachable, particularly during the desert seasons. To be encouraged that weeping may endure for a night but joy comes in the morning.

To remain in steadfast faith as it gives me patience, drive, strength, wisdom, fortitude, grace, peace, joy and gratitude through the tough times. Faith also helps me to scale above the turbulence and waves of change.

It is often said that faith helps one in the journey to becoming everything they were meant to be. Particularly while on a journey of self-mastery. A journey of self-leadership. And while on a journey of self-control. Furthermore, while in pursuit of health, wealth, spiritual, mental and social growth.

To be aware of the enemy within and without. To be adaptable. |To embrace change. To reinvent self where need arises. To appreciate that opportunities may come camouflaged as challenges and or struggles.

As a word of caution, to not expect to be automatically successful. To believe and work towards success. As witnessed in John 5:6, Jesus asks the man who has been lame for 38 years "Do you want to get healed?" The sick man answered "Sir, I have no man to put me into the pool when the water is troubled, and while I am going, another steps down before me." Evidently, the sick man had resigned himself to his fate. He blamed his situation to having no support system around him. Jesus called on him to make best of what he had at his disposal and also to believe in a higher power. Similarly, the same is witnessed with Moses second guessing himself due to his stammer. In the both instances, the persons had to make best of what was available and also plug into a higher authority to be healed and confidently move forward.

To mind my attitude, as attitude is said to determine one's altitude. One may be stuck due to a negative attitude, they say. To appreciate the need for a mental detox of negative thought patterns. To refresh, refocus, restart and reboot if need be. What most would call a renewal of the mind and or paradigm shift. To take a leap into the ring. To not be a spectator. To make things happen. To claim what you want and start to expect that. To appreciate the need to put away the garbage in order to soar. To embrace lifelong spiritual healing through God's living waters.

Also, to not get stuck because of fear as fear kills hopes and dreams. Fear will hold me back. To end fear. To monitor my inner conversations. To be my own best friend. To be kind to myself. To be positive and have a positive mind-set. To guard my mind as there is nothing to fear but fear itself. To take courage.

To keep in mind that we all make mistakes that leave us devastated, humiliated, stressed, ashamed and hurt. Not to mention feelings of pain, of guilt, suffering, rejection, disappointment, betrayal and or stigma.

To choose not to be driven by the guilt and or the opinions of others. To hold my head up, to dust myself and forge forward.

To not let my mistakes, past, traumas, circumstances and or setbacks hold me back. To rise above my situation. To be encouraged by a common phrase that follows, "what does not kill you, will only make you stronger".

To stand up for yourself and take charge of my territory. To say no to negative thinking, vibes, stories, mind-set and or toxic environment. To take control of my emotions. To take note that negative emotions are like weeds, they choke the life out of you.

To identify what I need to change and schedule the change. To be aware of hurdles that I may have to overcome such as the urge for perfection, over analysis, overthinking, inner conflict, battle in the mind, lack of confidence, self-limiting mind-set, excuses, justification and or lack of resources. To constantly seek out opportunities for self-improvement.

To appreciate that I am a vessel and instrument for a higher purpose. Hence the need to be well prepared in order to bear fruit for the Kingdom. To harness the right attitude and relentlessly upskill to be of service to community.

To live up to and advocate for my desired value system. Have a set of values that I stand for. To take into account that my values will also inform my personal brand. That is, who I am and who I am not. To have set boundaries of my value system.

To be aware that the value system I stand for also informs my contribution. My value-add and or solution in the marketplace.

My service and or product packaging, positioning, personality, image and style should also match up.

IDEALLY, MY PRODUCT and or service offering should be different. An alternative. Ultimately, the product or service should provide a solution to a problem, empower, equip, inspire, enrich, encourage, educate, assist, make impact and or make a difference.

To have an action plan. It is said, not planning is planning to fail. To have a roadmap, set SMART (Specific, Measurable, Achievable, Realistic and Time bound) goals and work plan on how to achieve the goals.

To have a plan powered by vision, mission, a value statement, summary skillset, systems, structures and resources available. The key objective being to exceed the customer expectation.

To be intentional and deliberate when picking a team to work with. As a team may be necessary to execute the purpose. To prepare the team. To be a servant leader. To also consider mentors, coaches, advisors, partners, accountability partners, support systems, networks, associations and or collaborations that may propel my given purpose. Of importance, to pick a team that shares the same vision and value system. Also while on boarding, to consider persons who not only empower me but also inspire.

Further, of the need to keep a watchful eye on the environs inside out. To avoid distractions and or slipping back into a comfort zone. To remain steadfast throughout the journey.

On the other hand, to be on the lookout for haters, nay Sayers and frenemies. Like Jesus, to be aware that I may be persecuted by the world, but to be of good cheer, Jesus overcame and in Him, we are more than conquerors. To consistently review my environment and facets of life to establish the areas that need improvement. To be a lifelong student while remaining in the vine and not conforming to the ways of the world.

To be reminded that over time, my scorecard and or measure of success will be determined by the lives impacted. Others may liken it to legacy. That is, the result of serving and or providing a product.

Legacy is arguably how one would you want to be remembered or will be remembered. The contribution they made to the community. The baton that they passing forward. The contribution one has made towards the Kingdom's dominion and or multiplication. The tending made to God's sheep.

Granted, I should strive to be my brother's keeper and Kingdom's ambassador.

Like with Jesus, live in the hope that in the end, God will proclaim, "this is my child whom I am well pleased".

Treasure gems

- To be deliberate and intentional. Make things happen. To not wait for things to happen.
- To articulate my purpose, vision, mission, value statement, brand, positioning, roadmap, goals and if need be the qualified team.
- To keep in mind that someone else opinion of me does not have to be my reality. I am different, unique and have my own, one of a kind thumbprint. An original and not a perfect copy of someone else. I am a product of God's workmanship. A masterpiece. Am wonderfully and fearfully made. I am made in God's image. I am a child of the highest God.
- To watch out for what keeps me stuck. To watch my inner conversations, battle in the mind and conflicted beliefs as they will manifest in my own story and reflect on my self-value.
- To keep in mind that "I am who I am" regardless of my status and or circumstances. For as the good book professes, "As a man thinketh so is he".
- To interrogate my negative feelings such as anger, bitterness, resentment, low self-esteem, self-doubt, lacking confidence, fear, hopelessness, being lost, out of control, unworthiness, inadequacy, incapable, undeserving and or insecure and identify the basis of the feeling.
- To keep a watch of how I project or communicate my pain, hurt, inner struggle, fears and myriad of emotions. Whether directly and indirectly. Whether consciously and or unconsciously. Whether to self, abuser, perpetrator and or others. Whether physically, emotionally and or verbally.
- To process the feelings, evaluate the feelings and choose to respond

positively.

- To unpack baggage, Forgive, Reconcile, Make Peace and Love. To love and pray for my enemies.
- To drop the victim mentality. To own my healing process and soldier on.
- To appreciate that healing is arguably a lifelong process. To extend grace to myself and others.
- To let go and let God.
- To be proud of my scars, as the scars show courage to live on, to take risks and to experience what life has to offer.
- To live, learn, grow and share.
- To hold on to steadfast Faith and Hope.
- To be spiritually grounded.
- To be still and know God.
- To seek out God and trust that He will give me, my heart's desires in conformity with His will.
- To remember that God loves me and am priceless before Him.
- To not lose sight of my own true identity and belonging in Jesus Christ. As am redeemed and made righteous in Jesus Christ.
- To remain focused on the cross.
- To keep the gratitude up.
- To pray for grace.
- To also pray to be filled with the indwelling of the Holy Spirit whose fruit is love, joy, peace, fortitude, kindness, goodness and faithfulness.
- To embrace change, self-improvement, growth and transformation.
- To be teachable and humble.
- To keep a keen watch on what I confess, for there is power in the tongue.
- To be authentic.
- To serve others from a place of Love and not from a selfish agenda.
- To adopt purpose, a new mind-set, new attitude, positive value system, peace, love and joy.
- To find my true north, fulfil God's will, bear fruit, add value, alleviate pain and be a problem solver.
- People will mostly remember how you made them feel. To treat people

well, to appreciate, encourage, support and make others feel like they matter.

- To pray to God for His guidance as you pursue your purpose, vision, goals, hopes, dreams, desires, aspirations, passions and interests.
- To Make Specific Measurable Achievable Realistic and Time bound goals.
- To remember, that I can do all things through Christ who strengthens me.
- Not to fear failure. To fail forward. To be inspired by Confucius quote, "that our greatest glory is not in never falling but in rising every time we fall".
- To commit to value-add. Be intentional and deliberate of the fruit I bring to the table.
- To invite accountability partners.
- Overall, to make my life and that of others matter. To empower, make an impact, make a difference, inspire, enrich and light up the world.
- To be indeed the change I want to see in the world.